To Andrea
With every good wish

"It is very well written and is an important statement on a growing problem.

"It was rewarding to me to renew my acquaintance with the teachings of Deuteronomy, a Biblical book which has had a great influence in my life. I liked your handling of the religious aspect of loneliness."

James A. Michener

"Its utter candor, forthrightness and warmth cannot fail to move the reader . . . I realize how much pain it must cause to those who experience it, and I am glad that you are able and willing to offer comfort to them."

Professor Louis Finkelstein

"Dr. Mandelbaum makes a valuable contribution to the inspirational literature on recovery from loneliness . . . Particularly illuminating is his application of the function of the Sabbath to the process of recovery. *Calling on your own inner resources*—the Sabbath experience—speaks to people of all faiths."

David Peretz, M.D.
Department of Psychiatry
Columbia University

YOU ARE NOT ALONE

THE CONQUEST OF LONELINESS

**BERNARD
MANDELBAUM**

SHENGOLD PUBLISHERS, INC.
New York

ISBN 0-88400-132-6   0-88400-133-4 (PBK)
Library of Congress Catalog Card Number: 88-43148
Copyright © 1988 by Bernard Mandelbaum

Published by Shengold Publishers, Inc.
New York, N.Y.

Printed in the United States of America

For Judy who is still with me . . .

and Marcelle who has been my strength for the past three years.

Acknowledgments

The people to whom I owe so much for help in writing this volume are referred to in the pages ahead, notably my precious children—Joel, Dasi, David, Debra, and Naomi—and their wonderful families. Above all, my Judy, who was with me before and is with me now. And, thank God, for the past three years Marcelle has been my strength.

To these, let me add Kay Tacouni, who, while typing, helped with both criticism and encouragement at the right times. My "merciless" editor, Beverly Colman, who was so kind, and my publisher, Moshe Sheinbaum, who has always been a dear friend and an advisor of great wisdom.

Contents

Foreword

The very personal element in this book moves me to share with you, the reader, my purpose in writing it. After the tragic loss of Judith, my beloved wife of thirty-five years, I experienced the most painful, depressing loneliness. Despite some three years of almost total surrender to it, *I conquered loneliness*. Portraying the phases of my suffering, the path back to fullness of life—for life's *emptiness* is the very essence of the pain—the role of family, friends, doctors, and, above all, myself: all this, I believe, can be of help to others. That is my goal.

The contents in the pages ahead can be divided into two major parts: (1) Know thyself and your loneliness, and (2) Do something about.

The first part will detail the nature of loneliness and its various levels, from the most destructive to the initial rays of hope. The second part will be very specific about attitudes, actions, exercises—indeed, disciplines—that helped me overcome it.

The title of the book is another way of describing my purpose. It gives expression to a conviction on two levels. In practical terms of everyday life, "You Are Not Alone": you would be amazed to learn how many people out there are experiencing the anguish of loneliness. "The Conquest of Loneliness": many of these people licked the problem, and so can you.

Further, "You Are Not Alone" in what might be identified as "religious" terms. There is One God of all the world Who is always there to sustain it. With your better understanding of what this means and with the help of other people—and yourself, made in His image —you are sufficiently powerful and creative to bring about "The Conquest of Loneliness."

BERNARD MANDELBAUM

New York, January 1989

Introduction

Whenever I have been afraid that my work was so personal that no one could understand it, everybody did understand it. When I tried to speak to others, they didn't know what I was talking about.

—Mark Van Doren

I was not aware of it when it was happening. As I was planning the outline—and into the actual writing—I began to realize something that was, to me, most fascinating.

From the superb volumes of a Moustakas to some of the silliest books on the subject of loneliness, every one cited within these pages and many that I did not include, were a combination of research results and autobiography. This is what my book became. The combination of autobiography and research reflects that what was true of the other writers is certainly true of me: the compelling need to write this book comes as much from my inner "gut" as from my heart and mind.

This awareness gave me the support I needed. To describe the tragic loss of my wife would be much too difficult for me—much too personal. The reader will learn enough about these details in the succeeding chapters without my presenting them here separately. They are used specifically in context when they are part of the development of a greater understanding of loneliness. For I am absolutely certain that my experience—from sadness to misery; my reactions—fear and hope—are the emotions of most people who are shackled by loneliness. My hope is that the lessons I learned and tried to record in these pages will be helpful to others, from those who experience a deep loneliness to those who are on the edge.

1

Do You Recognize Yourself?

He who overcomes loneliness, overcomes his greatest enemy.

ANONYMOUS

"Why two eyes for vision?" a rabbi was asked by his disciple. "God could have arranged it with one." The rabbi replied, "One eye is to see the virtues in others; the other eye is to see the faults in yourself."

HASIDIC LORE

Why does a caricature of a person or event have great impact? Presenting something in extreme, even exaggerated terms forces us to see the real facts.

My description of loneliness is not a caricature. But I will present it, initially, in extreme form—at its worst—so that we can better recognize it in all its degrees. There are many, like myself, who know the meaning of loneliness from the depths of uncontrollable, extended years of mourning the loss of a wife or husband.

The immediate result of such a loss is a sense of *emptiness*. This is *the* key to understanding the nature of loneliness. When life is empty, you don't look forward to a rising sun; there is nothing new, no one interesting. Days and moments are a vacuum, without purpose, direction, or meaning. Existence is one continuous drudgery, where even the hoped-for relief of sleep is exhausting. A seemingly endless list of feelings comes to mind when I think about my own experience of loneliness and emptiness: depression, listlessness, self-doubt, uncertainty, impotence, no choices in life, inability to relate to anyone.

To demonstrate the many levels (or types) of loneliness, let's look at how it can occur where you would least expect to find it: in the college student.

"I'm sorry, Mom, but Vassar is not what you think it is. It isn't exciting and challenging. Quite the opposite.

It's . . . *Lonely*! And I'm not the only one who feels it. All the kids I know feel the same way. Believe me, that lovely, exciting and challenging school is the loneliest place in the world! Why, students hardly even nod at each other on campus. We don't sit around the dorm rapping, like those bull sessions you and Dad described from when you were in college, twenty-five years ago."

The parents stare at their daughter in disbelief. She continues: "Everyone is 'on the make,' but not the way we usually mean. True, the boys are on the make for girls and the girls are on the make for boys, and you wouldn't believe how many boys are on the make for boys and girls for girls! But worse, almost everyone is 'on the make' for better grades; to get 'in' with a professor to get a better grade or a job when they graduate. That's why everyone is wrapped up in his own world. They're all outdoing someone else. So what we have is this feeling of isolation, of loneliness. And you know, it scares me. I just want to get away from the whole scene."

How appropriate here is a line from Lawrence Stoddard's play *Alone Together*: "Maybe that's what growing up is; learning to be less afraid."

The daughter continues: "That's why I want to get out into the world for a year—the real world. To meet people, to travel see Europe. Maybe I could really use my French and Spanish. Those language courses seem so useless to me now. Everything does. But if I take off the year, maybe it would relieve this depressed feeling down deep; this . . . loneliness."

The parents helplessly see the tears welling up in their child's eyes and are unable to respond.

"I know," she goes on, "it may not be any better on the outside. But I must try."

There is an additional aspect to the true story of this college student: Parents—even the most intelligent and sophisticated—often don't have the slightest idea of what their children are thinking or feeling, whether at an out-of-town school or in their own rooms at home. This absence of relatedness or involvement with people—especially between parents and children— often can be the beginning of loneliness.

And again, lines from Stoddard's *Alone Together* point up the student's frustration. "MIT stands for 'Men in Trouble.' It's a veritable combat zone—an unfriendly, uptight place. Fourteen to one is the number of lows—according to Professor Buchanweidis—to a high. Six live in his apartment; the shades are always drawn. It's like an isolation booth—removed from everything."

To be "removed from everything" is an apt description of the feeling of loneliness. It is hard for someone who hasn't experienced it to imagine what this is like.

And generally it is the most difficult of tasks to put oneself in another's place:

> Don't judge [a person] until you are in his situation.

> In judging others, give them the benefit of the doubt.

These are two statements from the second-century *Ethics of the Fathers*. They reflect the centrality of this ideal in the Jewish ethos. It is taught in many different ways in rabbinic literature, underscoring how difficult it is to achieve.

As told in hasidic lore, two friends are at a bar with one drink too many. One asks the other:

"Are you my friend?"

"Of course I'm your friend! What kind of question is that?"

"Do you love me?"

"Come on, now, you know I love you."

"Do you know what hurts me?"

"*I* should know what hurts *you*? How can *I* know what hurts *you*?"

"Well, if you don't know what hurts me, how can you say you are my friend and that you love me?"

Indeed, it compounds the loneliness when there is no one you know who even begins to understand or can identify with your sense of isolation; when the relative, friend, or neighbor to whom you look for some sensitivity to your feelings has never had an experience remotely resembling yours. It is hoped that the reader will become aware of two purposes of these descriptions of loneliness: they should strike a responsive chord and lead to some hope for those who are experiencing it; those who, fortunately, have not, will, hopefully, become more sensitive to the lonely person and, at the least, be of help with an understanding heart.

The widespread presence of the problem is attested to by the writer John Gunther, who covered the length and breadth of this country in his research for one of his books and found that loneliness is "one of the supreme American problems." And what Gunther concluded in his travels, the psychiatrist Harry Stack Sullivan discovered in his probing into the makeup of contemporary man: "The problem in Freud's early decades was sexual repression . . . . [Today it is] loneliness, isolation and difficulty in self-esteem."

Some attention to the nuance of words and their meaning might be helpful. Perhaps, instead of "loneliness," the word we want is "lonesomeness." The bereaved widower is lonesome for someone dear who is missed; the college student is longing for a value, sense of purpose, or meaningful relationship which is missing.

It is also important to be clear about another aspect of loneliness. It isn't always all bad. Aloneness can be constructive and is an aspect of all creative experience. Moses was alone in the desert when he had a vision of God in the burning bush; Augustine was alone in his garden when he first sensed God's presence. Albert Einstein was a shy, "loner," which was probably a major factor in his coming upon his revolutionary theory of relativity. Later, especially in the chapter on the Sabbath, the creative aspects of aloneness and solitude will be developed. Our immediate task is to identify the variety of experiences of loneliness and its symptoms.

As indicated, it runs a full gamut, from the depression of someone in mourning to the sadness of a young person who finds no purpose, meaning, or human warmth in life. The loneliness of the college student at Vassar probably began at home, with the absence of any meaningful relationship with her parents. Note that her hope is to go out into the world to conquer loneliness; she does not expect to find it in returning home. Most young people—from "selfish" teenagers to our college student—can look forward to growing out of it with the formation of meaningful relationships and developing a purpose in life. Our special concern is for those who have reached maturity in years, when the loss of a dear one—through death or divorce or alienation—opens the abyss of loneliness.

We can better understand the rupture in personality

brought about by such losses if we appreciate the deeper meaning of love, never described more vividly than by, of all people, the philosopher-scientist Bertrand Russell:

> Love is something far more than the desire for sexual intercourse; it is the principal means of escape from loneliness which afflicts most men and women throughout the greater part of their lives . . . . Nature did not construct human beings to stand alone since they cannot fulfill their biological purpose except with the help of another; and civilized people cannot fully satisfy their sexual instinct without love.

Even when there is not the deeper experience of love between husband and wife, a marriage creates routines, patterns of predictable relationships. Not all marriages are terrific, but most provide such familiar, dependable patterns. When they are gone, there is an emptiness. They are terribly missed and bring about a loneliness even in people who are divorced after a marriage that, supposedly, offered no companionship.

From the breach of a deep love between husband and wife to the separation from a routine companionship, what are the feelings that take over and cause the oppressive loneliness? It doesn't hit you suddenly, like getting up with a headache. It grows and develops gradually. Not surprisingly, it is the product of a quality of life in our times that has been described as "fragmentation"—life is like a patchwork quilt, with no continuity of purpose. There may be colorful moments, but they have no depth of meaning and are not related to one another. There is a sense of "Where am I? . . . What's happening to me?"

The loneliness to which this leads seldom stands still on one level for long. It either begins to lift slowly, or it deepens and leads to thoughts and sometimes acts of suicide. Consider: into which of the following categories do you fit, or into what combination?

1. *A gnawing, almost subliminal sense of despondency.* The pain is bearable. It just doesn't seem right. This can't be what living is about—a dullness and a mild, continuous sadness. It is all such a waste.

The one thing we have been given is time. To permit it to pass in even mild unpleasantness is to "kill time." This is a partial suicide.

2. *A general feeling of impatience and tendency to fly off the handle.* You may not be content with what life seems to have meted out to you. There is no companionship or friendship to speak of. Therefore, you lack someone with whom to share your hopes and frus-

trations. You tend to blame everyone around you; thus your impatience with others, especially their problems. You live with the illusion that some outside force —"life"—is determining what is happening to you rather than realize how much you and your attitude shape the quality of your days. This makes you short-tempered and quick to pick on everyone and everything around you. Often you just feel like crying . . . and sometimes you do.

Significantly, these are not only the experiences of a widow or widower, divorced person, or one who has never been married. Married people, with all the externals of a mate—as a "lover" and "friend"—can feel and react this way.

3. *Deep depression.* This is a feeling of actual pain caused by the intense sadness.

In a superb volume, *Conquering Loneliness*, the psychiatrist Jean Rosenbaum and his wife, Veryl, a psychologist, detail specific "symptoms" of this malady called loneliness.

Do you recognize yourself? Have you heard yourself saying these words?:

"No one will *ever* care for me."

"I can't go on. I feel so alone."

And even when you are out with friends, whether

just visiting or attending a party, the depression and alienation remain with you—sometimes more so. You often feel as if you are a fifth wheel.

The Rosenbaums also describe what is both a cause and symptom of loneliness:

> Your self-critical eye is constantly seeking situations to prove to you how unworthy you are, to keep you enslaved in loneliness . . . . Are you as critical of your acquaintances as you are of yourself? If this is the case, then you *are* in trouble.

Other descriptions come from *In Search of Intimacy*, by Rubenstein and Shaver:

> It's a desperate longing . . . like a hole or space in the middle of my body, a wound. And I can feel it all the time. Even when I'm with another person, it's there, sort of waiting to grow later on, when I'm alone.

> A pain in the chest—almost literally a broken heart.

> I come home from work feeling empty. I try to tell myself that my projects are going well—and they are. But after a while, that just isn't worth much. What good is success if there's nobody around to appreciate it . . . and to share it with.

In her book, *Bittersweet: Surviving and Growing from Loneliness*, Terri Shultz writes from the innards of her own experience and anguish:

> The loneliness of living by yourself can be terrifying. I was reminded of this once when I was lying on a sunny rock and saw a small crab inches away, hurtling across the rocks as if it were on fifty legs. If we humans could run as fast for our size, we wouldn't need jets, I thought. But when confronted with loneliness it is as if I, too, sprout legs and zoom away. That is how fast and frantic I am as I scurry from it, from emptiness. But when you live alone, where do you scurry to? Sometimes I feel like the crab on the rock; I run for my life from the giant shadows that loom over me.

> Sometimes this loneliness of my solitary life is comfortable, and sometimes it is like a dull pain, and sometimes the loneliness is like hanging on to a cliff by the fingernails and I claw and kick my way back to safety, using all my strength.

"I claw and kick my way back to safety, using all my strength" indicates the sense of determination needed by the lonely person. It is good advice for the next steps in this confrontation with loneliness.

There are those who can fully identify with the pain described above; others may feel at the very edge of it; still others may wonder whether this could ever happen to them. Facing the reality of these feelings is the first step in dealing with them. The next two chapters will be very specific and concrete in dealing with what you can do about it. However, one conviction underlies all the advice: the power that you, the individual, have to do something about it. You must never use the excuse that "what I do doesn't make a difference."

2

Insights on Loneliness from the Bible and Jewish Thought

It is not good for man to be alone.

GENESIS 2:18

Hillel teaches: Do not withdraw from the community.

ETHICS OF THE FATHERS 2:5

It is easy to identify with the conviction expressed by Abraham Lincoln in the turmoil of his relationship with his wife. "To remain as I am is impossible. I must die or *be better*" [emphasis added].

How often did I have this thought in the morass of my loneliness! An insight that came to me after three years of suffering is expressed in a medieval text: "What time does [in healing] no wisdom can achieve." This is not a license for doing nothing when faced with a problem. "In time things will straighten out" is *not* a formula for meaningful living. On the contrary, a person, viewed as a partner with God, is encouraged to take on his or her responsibility and do something with the expectation that there can be good results. However, the text is calling for a posture which a person, struggling against loneliness, has to understand: the importance of patience, keeping at it and not giving up despite the two steps forward and then perhaps one step backward until you hit your stride. And slowly but surely, in this step-by-step process, you put destructive loneliness behind you.

Healing comes in stages with different levels of loneliness. In the earliest period of deep depression, there was very little that I could do. A day consisted of reading the *New York Times* from the first page to the last, rotely, with very little really registering. Television played a role, although it seldom did more than fill time.

Slowly—with the help of my children and good friends—I began to emerge from the cocoon of my small apartment. Convinced that action, as well as attitude, is important, I literally forced myself to relate to people, to be in the company of others. I took the bull by the horns and made my first date, after three years of fearing it. On the date, I kept wondering, "What am I doing here?" There I was, with someone whose company I admittedly was enjoying, yet I felt so isolated, so alone. And the feeling of guilt: "I am being disloyal to Judy."

I had always heard and believed, and even taught: "Only a happily married person seeks out a second marriage." And I had been very happily married! "This date," I kept telling myself, "is a compliment to Judy, so why do I feel so alienated . . . and guilty?"

As with many a pronounced principle, it looks good on paper, in the textbooks, in the psychiatrist's office. But the heart's reaction is beyond reason. In the company of a date or at a social function, you find yourself most lonely. It is a kind of numb loneliness rather than a depressed one.

To understand the slow process of overcoming loneliness, we are aided by a contrast: the bright side—the ability of people to live alone *without* feeling loneliness. The full recognition of this can be a major step toward dispersing the dark clouds of loneliness.

I was privileged to know just such a "bright-sided" person. She was Mrs. Ida Perlberg, my Judy's grandmother. (We called her "Bubie," Yiddish for grandmother.) A television program on her life, "Mrs. Perlberg's Partner in Heaven," had the following scene, reflecting her outlook and typical of many a pious person of her generation:

> *One of her children telephones her:*
> FRIEDA: Good morning, Mamma. You answered
> the phone? Isn't Gertie home with You?
> Are you alone?
> BUBIE: Never alone!

Clearly this is what the psalmist had in mind in the twenty-third chapter: "Yea, though I walk in the valley of the shadow of death . . . Thou art with me."

Not many of us today are blessed with this total, unswerving faith in God's immanence and nearness to us. Bubie's answer, however, suggests a truth for even the most "devout" secularist who does not believe in God. For him, it is important to find his own secular package of values, ideals, and commitments, for to "feel alone" is to be *empty* of content and purpose in life. This unhappy state is vividly described in Johne Osborn's novel *Look Back in Anger*, in which a young man bitterly laments the emptiness of life where "all beliefs, all convictions, all enthusiasms have vanished." How much better if we could all view life as he does:

> For me, there is something ineffably new in every moment's arriving. And even things I habitually do, have qualities new and surprising. There's nothing that happens that happened before in exactly that way in my life.

> Emptiness in a person does not stay for long, and demands to be filled, and is often infiltrated by loneliness.

> And I think of what an enormous opportunity it is to be alive on this planet. Having myself been cold and hungry and terribly alone, I think I still feel the excitement of that opportunity.

Returning for a moment to those who have the ability to recognize God as a force in life, even amongst them, there are differences about how God is viewed in His response to man. In Jewish tradition, an individual is considered a partner with God in shaping the character of his life and the destiny of the world. "Why wasn't man born circumcised, if it is such a good thing?" the Midrash asks. And it answers, "God said to man, I have created you up to this point, and now you, as My partner, finish the job with the circumcision of man.'"

It is my conviction that accepting this relationship of each of us with God makes the conquest of loneliness easier. And He can be found anywhere. Commenting on those who say that Jacob succeeded in feeling close to God at the top of the ladder because the earth on which he stood was holy ground, the nineteenth century British writer John Rusk observed that any place may be the place that God lets down the ladder. The challenge is: Are we ready to grasp the rungs? Only the lonely person himself can know when he is ready, and only he can grasp the rungs of the ladder that will enable him to climb out of the depths of his isolation and despair. It is not an easy job and demands prodigious effort.

The heroic Helen Keller gives vivid expression to what a supreme effort is involved:

> I who am blind can give hint to those who see. Use your eyes as if tomorrow you would be stricken blind. *And the same method can be applied to your other senses.* [Emphasis added]

> Hear the music of voices, the song of a bird, the mighty strains of an orchestra as if you would be stricken deaf tomorrow. Touch each object as if

tomorrow your tactile sense would fail. Smell the perfume of flowers, taste with relish each morsel—as if tomorrow you would never smell and taste again. Glory in all these facets of pleasure and beauty which the world reveals to you: Make the most of your senses!

To these wise and courageous words, I add that there is a sixth sense which is reflected in the faith expressed by Bubie. There is no question that my faith played an important role and provided the rungs of the ladder which enabled me to climb up from the abyss of depression. Fortunately, I was able to climb pretty high. I received a poem from a young friend, David Goodbaum, when I lost Judy:

She Is . . .

Do not stand at her grave and weep.
She is not there. She does not sleep
She is a thousand winds that blow.
She is the diamond glint on the snow.
She is the sunlight on the ripened grain.
She is the gentle autumn rain.
When you awake in the morning's hush,
She is the swift uplifting rush
Of quiet birds in circled flight.

She is the brilliant stars that shine at night.
Do not stand at her grave and weep.
She is not there.
She did not die.

This was a seed of thought completely hidden within me during the years of sadness. However, as I began my way back on the path of living, it flowered into a deep conviction about the meaning of immortality. "Search not for what is hidden from you" is good advice from Ben Sirah, the author of Ecclesiasticus. Yet human growth and society's progress have been the result of such searching. And it is in the moment of pain and sorrow that we are most inclined to give thought to the deeper realities. Thus, my mind has been occupied with the ways Judy continues to live.

Again, in the words of Ben Sirah, "A good name lives forever" and Judy's lives on as a continuing influence in our children and grandchildren, her parents and brother, her cousin, friends, co-workers, and patients. "Her strength, her understanding and grace made a deep impression on me and I admired her greatly. I will miss all the wonderful insights that touched me, through my friendship with Dasi." This letter from my daughter's friend demonstrates that Judy's influence reached even beyond those directly in contact with her.

But, I wanted something more than that: Judy, herself, living in the World to Come while I continue to feel her presence here and now. And as I seek, I do, indeed, find her in all of us in the family; sometimes in people I have just met. My conviction that she literally lives on today arises from my conclusion that there is a plan in the universe that comes from the Creator.

While one should not be overoccupied with what is "beyond you," the mind keeps working; the heart feels and the soul believes. Just as humanity, made in God's image, is urged to imitate His ways (of mercy, kindness), so, too, must this world, which God created for us, be a microcosm of all God's creations. Therefore, by understanding how things happen in this world, we get a glimpse into "what is hidden from us." We can then begin to see His overall plan.

To plan, implies continuity, something ongoing. God's plan for Creation has such continuity built into it.

If, in New York City, we want to go from First Avenue and First Street to Tenth Street and Fourth Avenue, we go three blocks west and nine blocks north. This clear course is possible because a "creator" of the city's *plan* of streets arranged it. Suppose, however, that whoever laid out the city streets did so by taking numbers one through twelve (for avenues) and one through two hundred and forty (for the streets), and then scrambled these numbers and designated the streets arbitrarily, unplanned. Would we get to our destination—if at all—except after a long, hit-and-miss process?

How simple is a little city, even New York City, in comparison to the universe. Yet scientists can send a rocket into space, traveling for over ten years, covering billions of miles, and at an appointed time, it lands on its exact target in the heavens. Could this be achieved if the world happened accidentally, if it were a scramble of phenomena? Therefore, the most advanced scientific achievements of the space program affirm a planned creation of the universe.

Based on Einstein's belief in the uniformity and harmony of nature, scientific research today has as its goal a universal theorem known as the Unified Field Theory. The implication is that the time will come when *one* theorem—for example, x = 2y—will describe the relationship of forces that are explored in all the sciences: chemistry, physics, electronics, etc. Indeed, the Nobel Prize winners in physics for 1984 were given the award for advancing the validity of the Unified Field Theory.

For those of us who accept the basic insights of the Bible, this is not surprising. The same One God created heaven and earth according to His plan, and heaven and earth are the locales where science operates. More and more, scientific discoveries point to a plan for the world, indeed the universe, leading to the inevitable conclusion that it was planned by the Creator.

In such a plan, it follows that the goodness and wisdom of Judy don't get lost accidentally and must continue. How? In what form? These are questions for which there are no direct answers. In the words of King David about his son who died, "I shall go to him, but he will not return to me." This is what Ben Sirah identifies as things that "have been shown more than you can understand." However, it is my conviction that we have been shown enough to lead to the inevitable conclusion that Judy lives on in the presence of our Maker, at the same time that she continues in each of us.

Our son, David, received his medical degree several weeks after Judy's death. He had of course been visiting her regularly, and on one of these occasions, he said, "You know, Mom, we celebrated Passover here at the hospital and Purim, too. So again, after the commencement exercises on May 24th, we'll all come here for a party."

"David," she replied firmly, "I will *be* there!"

On the day Judy left us, David said, "She must have known. There is only one way she could have been there. This way." We, the family, are all convinced that she was there—and experienced still another moment of joy and fulfillment—added to all the other such moments given to her by Joel, Dasi, David, Debra and Naomi.

There is a tradition that comes from ancient China via modern Japan that demonstrates an insight we could learn from. Just as we, in the West, designate "things"—paintings, monuments, buildings—as special treasures, they designate certain people as *Living Treasures*. Judy was . . . no, *is*, a Living Treasure. And so, to Joel's concluding words of his eulogy, "Ma, we'll miss you," I add . . . "even though we know that you are there and here—with us."

These convictions were a tremendous help to me in combating the sense of loneliness created by Judy's death, but they do not complete the job. I am still lonely for her.

Can you, the reader—the lonely person—identify with all this? Does it help at all? Perhaps, somewhat. For if it doesn't do the total job for me, a person who believes this deeply, how can it lighten the burden of loneliness for someone who does not have this abiding faith? Perhaps it helps a little—a few flashes of responsive feeling and insight.

It is not, under any circumstances, an easy road the lonely must travel. There is a great deal of uncertainty along this path of progress toward eliminating loneliness, just as there is uncertainty in any experience of growth and development. In a private conversation with Rabbi Schneerson, the Rebbe of Lubavitch, he made this point: "In climbing a ladder, as the foot reaches from a lower rung to a higher one, there is, inevitably, a moment of uncertainty when the foot is in empty space before it lands securely on the higher rung."

This being so, a key factor for the lonely person trying to help himself is a series of convictions that must be assumed and reiterated, indeed cultivated until they are part of you, so that they sustain you when there is a discouraging moment. And many such moments will occur for the struggling lonely person, when there is doubt in his mind that progress is being made.

This power of one's mental attitude is confirmed by something of which more and more people are now aware: the direct relationship between attitudes of mind and the actual physical responses of the body. Having been edified on a popular level by Norman Cousins's *Anatomy of an Illness* many people now find some acceptance for what I and my family were planning if Judy had survived her fourth operation for cancer: a visit to a doctor of "holistic medicine."

Holistic medicine brings together the patient and his entire family for an uninterrupted twenty-four-hour period of talk and the airing of feelings. There is evidence that this has extended the years of cancer patients, although it is by no means a cure. It seems to me that the most diehard skeptics about this relationship between inner feelings and the body can be won over by reading a remarkable book by James J. Lynch, *The Broken Heart: The Medical Consequence of Loneliness*. Dr. Lynch goes into great detail about the relationship between loneliness, divorce, and heart attacks, and the differences between the responses of men and women.

I have been describing the development of ideas and attitudes that helped in my battle with loneliness. The lonely person dealing with his own despondency or someone on the edge, trying to prevent it, who reads this book may well be saying to himself: "All this is interesting and strikes many a responsive chord, *but what do you do?*" Chapter 5 will be very specific about concrete acts and disciplines which can alleviate and eliminate the depression of loneliness and helped save my life (because it was a kind of living death). However, the next paragraph is basic and gets to the very heart of the matter.

Ideas are the most powerful forces in life. They shape each of us as individuals, as well as the world in which we live. Ideas are active; to think a certain way is not a passive experience. "The greatest deeds are thoughts."

In summary, the ideas I have shared with you until now are part of the *actions* that are indispensable to eliminate loneliness. The next two chapters, also describing ideas and attitudes, are not dealing just with theories. They are *active steps* in eliminating loneliness and returning to a life that can be meaningful, even profound, and decent, even noble. The wisdom to be learned from great philosophers can be concretely helpful. The insight to be derived from the way Jews observe the Sabbath has significance for all people—regardless of their religious orientation—who seek help in pulling themselves up from the depression of loneliness.

3

Guidelines from Philosophers
over the Ages

*The world one lives in is determined by the
type of person one is.*

JOHANN GOTTLIEB FICHTE

I have met the enemy and he is us.

POGO

"The world one lives in is determined by the type of person one is." This simple but penetrating insight by the philosopher Johann Gottlieb Fichte explains why the world of the lonely person is so miserable and depressing. The statement was made in the eighteenth century. It reflects how philosophers over the ages, even when not directing themselves to the condition of loneliness, can throw light on the causes, conditions, and cures for it.

One can learn many lessons from what the great philosophers teach, even from their contradictions and mistakes. The great Aristotle, whose *Ethics* taught us the wisdom of the "golden mean" (the middle way) and who in his *Poetics* was the first to focus on the role of catharsis in drama—as in life generally—yet erred appallingly in one area. He teaches the most primitive of concepts, which could paralyze every lonely person.

In the *Ethics*, Aristotle teaches that man has choices and can shape his own character, be master of his own destiny. Yet, according to him, a slave is in such a status because of *his very nature*. His physical and mental structure determines that he is a slave—and nothing can change him. Aristotle was convinced that there is an area in the human condition which is predetermined and unchangeable. From this, the miser, the misanthrope—indeed, the lonely person—could be tempted to use the excuse: "It is my nature and there is nothing I can do about it."

The very opposite can be derived from Plato's *Republic*. Despite his controlled, authoritarian plan for forging the ideal state, Plato's idea for creating the philosopher-king implies our freedom and ability to shape character and disposition. It takes lifelong training and discipline to fashion such an ideal statesman. Implication: It is possible for a person to change a mood, frame of mind. It is, simply put, "doable."

In the Middle Ages, the distinguished Jewish philosopher Moses Maimonides, influenced by Aristotle, introduced his major work on Jewish law with a section on human character. A simple summary of what he would advise the lonely person is this: In pulling yourself out of the extreme of sadness, don't make the mistake of expecting to achieve utter joy. The best way is usually the "golden mean." And it takes tremendous effort, hitting and missing, to find the proper middle way.

Before continuing this exercise in seeming erudition, it should be clear to the reader that I have a purpose: to show that most of the great minds conclude that we can do something about our condition. Religious thinkers from the time of Moses, to the most naturalist, pragmatic of philosophers—William James and John Dewey—despite their fundamental differences, are in agreement on one principle: A person has tremendous control over what he is and what he can become; one can change. The choice of life or death (or a "living death") is in our hands. There is no basis for the excuse "What I do doesn't make a difference." On the contrary, while relatives and friends can help a person dispel the clouds of loneliness, the key force in rising above the misery, sadness, and boredom of loneliness rests with the person himself.

Francis Bacon (1561–1626) is usually considered the initiator of modern science. Descartes and others who followed affirmed the power of man to control nature and act in a way that would "ease man's estate." They stressed man's capacity to make a difference in determining the quality of his own life and society. I view this aspect of modern philosophy as another directive to our concern, the lonely person: "You *can* make a difference."

However, their emphasis on man's freedom to act did not eliminate the recognition of a moral structure built into the universe. The "categorical imperative" of Immanuel Kant is part of his view that the *duties* of a person are to be cultivated from earliest childhood. This requires hard work, sacrifice, persistence, determination. However, the world is so structured, with man at its center, that results can be achieved. When such great minds insist upon this power in everyman's mind, then the lonely person has to feel encouraged that he can face his problem with the expectation of change in himself.

It should also be a source of strength to know that an entire school of British empiricists, beginning with John Locke and George Berkeley, stress the power of man to determine his own nature and the quality of the society and the world in which he lives. According to Locke, we are born as a *tabula rasa*, a blank tablet, with no built-in inclinations or natural dispositions. Berkeley then carries this concept even further by suggesting that reality itself—even a chair or a tree— doesn't exist unless it is "created," as it were, in the human mind.

For our purposes, it is sufficient to see the clear guideline: You *do* make the crucial difference in what you are like, how you feel, and what becomes of your life.

This is equally true of the teaching of a group of American philosophers known as pragmatists, which includes John Dewey and William James. Dewey's view of *Human Nature and Conduct* (one of his books) is rooted in his judgment about the implication of the "miracles" of science. Progress is inevitable and one must be open to the new, which is always happening. This is, indeed, the very warp and woof of a philosophy that is uniquely American: there is nothing we cannot achieve.

Such an outlook errs in its near-worship of the new and often the implied denegration of ancient wisdom and traditional values. A case can be made that this view of life is the thrust that led to the complete relativism and self-indulgent morality of an Ernest Hemingway: "What is good is what you feel good after; what is bad is what you feel bad after."

Rejecting this hedonistic, self-indulgent concept of what is good can serve as an important parameter for the lonely person seeking his way back to normal living. "Normal living" is not without pain and suffering precious losses, and never really getting over them. It is naive to measure the elimination of loneliness by the extent to which joy is achieved. The good life is the difficult balance between extremities of mood.

The brevity of this chapter on what we can learn from philosophers and its location between a chapter on Jewish wisdom and one on the Sabbath reflect a conviction of mine which, by now, is no secret: Judaism, although rooted in a specific tradition, speaks to all people. Its insights into man and his world have influenced the thinking of Western civilization. Just as the basic values of democracy and freedom are rooted in the ethos of the Bible, philosophers who have probed human nature and conduct have been nurtured by this classic source. Included in such universal understanding of man is how to deal with loneliness. Thus, I introduce the next chapter about the Sabbath with a statement that will be repeated in context: "You don't have to be Jewish to learn lessons about loneliness, and life generally, from the Sabbath."

4

The Sabbath and Dispelling
the Clouds of Loneliness

*All his hideous doubt, despair and dark
confusion of the soul a lonely man must
know, for he is united to no image save that
which* he creates himself, *he is bolstered
by no other knowledge save that which* he
can gather for himself *with the vision of his
own eyes and brain. [Emphasis added]*

—Thomas Wolfe

*Three acts denote the seventh day: He
rested, He blessed, and He hallowed the
seventh day (Genesis 2:2–3). To the prohibition of labor is, therefore, added the
blessing of delight and the accent of sanc-
tity. Not only the hands of man celebrate
the day, the tongue and the soul keep the
Sabbath. One does not talk on it in the same
manner in which one talks on weekdays.
Even thinking of business or labor should
be avoided.* —Abraham Joshua Heschel

"More than the Jews protect (observe) the Sabbath, the Sabbath protects the Jews." What sounds like a rather parochial statement about Jews and one of their religious observances happens to offer tremendous insight which can enhance the life of all people, especially those caught in the morass of loneliness.

Many people, perhaps especially those Jews who are not particularly religious, think of the Sabbath as a day of "don'ts": don't work, don't watch television, don't shop, don't drive your car, don't answer the phone, etc. When properly observed, the Sabbath is actually a series of do's:

Do spend time with your family.

Do read, study, and reflect.

Do spend time at worship.

This means, then, occupy your time during this day, not with other worldly concerns, but rather by calling on *your own inner resources* to live with meaning here on earth.

In this context, the purpose of the laws of the Sabbath is to deepen and enrich life:

> The Sabbath is not dedicated exclusively to spiritual goals. It is a day of the soul as well as the body; comfort and pleasure are integral parts of the Sabbath observances: *Man in his entirety* must share in the blessing. [Emphasis added]   *Heschel*

The prohibition in Jewish law on the use of a car, television, telephone, or radio is part of one objective: to let us have an experience that is independent of machines and external assistances. Can you imagine a twenty-four-hour period with the phone not ringing once? Clearly, it would drive some people crazy—those who become restless and frightened when not endlessly "busy."

A most sensitive, inspired volume on the subject is Clark K. Moustakas's *Loneliness,* which defines this unhappy state so well. The following makes direct contact with anyone who has experienced loneliness to some degree, which means . . . everyone!

The loneliness of modern life may be considered in two ways: *The existential loneliness* which inexorably is a part of human experience and the *loneliness of self-alienation and self-rejection* which is not loneliness but a vague and disturbing *anxiety.*

Existential loneliness is an intrinsic and organic reality of human life in which there is both pain and triumphant energy out of long periods of desolation. In existential loneliness, man is fully aware of himself as an isolated and solitary individual, while in loneliness anxiety, man is separated from himself as a feeling and knowing person. [Emphasis added]

For a person struggling to rise from the pain of "anxiety loneliness" to the creativity of "existential loneliness," there is no better training ground than the rules of the Sabbath. The rules in the Christian tradition are not as detailed as those for the Jewish Sabbath, but all the Sunday Blue Laws in several of our states are rooted in religious observance. They are all directed toward putting a person in touch with himself; for example, the use of liquor could be a distraction, which is why it cannot be purchased in some states on Sunday.

Attendance at public worship is part of the Sabbath. The requirement to be with others in a community of worship, the usual get-together after services for the blessing over wine, the afternoon class, and visits to the homes of neighbors offer the very involvement with others which is the greatest need of the lonely person.

Time with the family is encouraged, from the opening-night home service which introduces the holy day (the father sings chapter 31 of Proverbs in praise of his wife, who is "the best in the world," and blesses the children).

At the same time, there are many elements of meaningful solitude: in study and even the almost required afternoon nap. As the Talmud says, "A Sabbath nap is a special delight."

The challenge, according to Rabbinic literature, is to extend a "taste" of the Sabbath throughout the week. In the busiest of days and most complicated of schedules, time must be found to stop the running and distractions and catch up with one's inner self. In Thomas Mann's words, "Solitude gives birth to the original in us, to beauty unfamiliar and perilous."

Miami Beach, the scene (perhaps the stereotype) of twentieth-century man's most frenetic activity, is also the locale for a delightful story about the late Professor Abraham Heschel. He was asked to lecture at an academic convocation in a synagogue and was given a room in the Fountainbleau Hotel. Overwhelmed by the luxury of its appointments and the proliferation of services and stores, he picked up his phone and asked the operator, "Would you be good enough to tell me on which floor is the library?"

Indeed, the "book"—man's ability to sit and read—is the antidote to what Moustakas refers to as the "individual in Western culture [who] often suffers from a dread of loneliness." And the book to which I refer is not only the Bible, the Prayer Book, the New Testament, the Koran. Earlier, when Bubie described herself as "never alone," we considered the "secular package" of content and meaning needed by those who do not have the simple, unquestioning faith of a Bubie.

The *Ethics of the Fathers*, a second-century text,

details a series of paradoxes that characterize a person with the inner strength to avoid anxiety and loneliness. One of the questions asked by Rabbi Tarfon is, "Who is a strong man?" The usual, expected answer would be in terms of one who governs others. Rabbi Tarfon's answer is: "The strong person is one who has power over *himself*" [emphasis added]. Thus, the really powerful, *active* person is one who can sit quietly in a chair and enjoy reading a book. He is not driven by forces beyond his control. *He* is in charge.

Such taking hold of oneself and doing things—step by step—to resist falling into the sense of hopelessness or lack of control which characterizes loneliness can begin to dispel the clouds. The Sabbath focuses on this and the *good things* to be experienced in this world. Reference to the Sabbath as a holy day (second only in importance to Yom Kippur, the "Sabbath of Sabbaths") should not mislead the reader to think of it as a matter of "otherworldly" concerns.

> One of the most distinguished words in the Bible is "*kadosh*," holy. What is the first holy object in the history of the world? Was it a mountain? Was it an altar?
>
> It is indeed a unique occasion at which the distinguished word "*kadosh*" is used for the first time: In the Book of Genesis, at the end of the story of

creation . . . it is applied to *time.* "And God blessed
the seventh day and made it holy" (Genesis 2:3).

Heschel

The Sabbath "stresses *holiness in time,* to be
attached to social events, to learn to consecrate sanc-
tuaries that emerge from the magnificent stream of the
year." The Talmud: "There are years which are filled
with life; there are years empty of life." And a year is an
accumulation of moments.

A person destroys the moments and years of his life
in many ways. Death itself is the cause of less pain than
the continuous anguish suffered by those who experience a living death—a bored, aimless succession of day
after day without meaning or excitement. Is there anything more revealing than some of the leisure activity
of people who talk about "killing time"?

It is amazing how man has used his ingenuity to
eliminate the values that enhance life and has substi-
tuted forces that are self-destructive. The Age of Reason that began in the eighteenth century stressed our
precious capacity to think. In the process, however, it
reasoned away a basic understanding of God and His
meaning for life as a whole. This has been given ulti-
mate expression as the "death of God." Life risks
becoming devoid of any long-range, deeper meaning.
The context of being is narrowed to whatever a person
can touch or feel or see or do *now,* immediately. We

often fool ourselves into thinking that we are planning for future years, but when they come we experience the same emptiness. The consequence of all this is the "death of man." "We make machines which act like men and produce men who act like machines."

Even more ominous for our individuality than the leveling process of technology is the commodity by which we measure our success: "That which exists for me through the medium of *money*, that which I can pay for, that I *am*, the possessor of money. The properties of money are my own properties and faculties. What I *am* and *can do* is, therefore, not all determined by my individuality" [emphasis added].

Opposing the forces of the machine and money, which reduce us to robotlike nonentities, is the biblical view of the human being who is made in God's image —a thinking, feeling, creative being with the possibilities of continuous renewal. The Sabbath is one of the most powerful instruments in the tradition to create such renewal. And it is such renewal that is the greatest need of the lonely person.

The one commodity available to all people—more precious than money or the things that money can buy —is the *time* we are given. Yet we squander this blessing. Time lies heavily on our hands. And having a television set in each room hasn't helped much. We kill time by running from one hobby to another, but these diversions soon lose their appeal. Even, and perhaps especially, the affluent are not any better off. They soon learn that the mad pace to accumulate things and the hot pursuit of activity in so-called leisure time are not in themselves sustaining, satisfying experiences.

Paradoxically, *man has a concern for immortality, but often does not know what to do on a free Sunday afternoon*. We have lost the ability to derive meaning from reflection and probing our inner resources. It has become difficult to derive joy from significant relations with other people. We are unable to derive strength and purpose from a sense of closeness to God. Yet we have been given time—the years of our life—to pursue these experiences which are unique to us as human beings.

What is life if not a stream of moments, days, weeks, months, years? What we do with these determines the quality, indeed, the length of our days. And how often is life like an empty, dark corridor through which we pass, rather than a bright expanse where the fullness of existence can be experienced?

There is no aspirin to relieve a headache of frustration and inner pain, nor are there any panaceas or gimmicks for adding years to our life. The life of an individual, or of a society, will not be maintained creatively by new gadgets or some new political arrangement. Our civilization and our lives can only improve if we choose to live by the basic truths already known to us. It is an evasion of responsibility to wait and hope for some new, magical revelation in the future to guide us to live, instead of using the insights, traditions, and resources available to us now. They are the best "medicines" available to treat loneliness.

That this takes hard work is stressed in an interesting blessing in the Jewish morning liturgy which gives thanks to God for the commandment to study Torah (the religious literature of Judaism). It does *not* conclude ". . . to study Torah," as the beginning of it would indicate, but instead, "to go about the business of studying the words of Torah." Why to "go about the *business*" instead of just "to study"? The commentary of Rabbi Isaac Finkelstein: "If we were to go about the study of the Torah with the same persistence, readiness to work hard, as we go about building our business, we would derive the proper guidelines for ordering our life in a meaningful and creative way."

The Talmud states that, in the World to Come, a person will have to give an accounting of why he deprived himself of a pleasure he could have legitimately enjoyed. The joys of the world—family, friendship, music, art, reading, athletics—are exactly what the discouraged, lonely person should be thinking about. He should try to use them as a major step in pulling himself out of the morass of his anxiety and depression.

Again, you don't have to be Jewish or a Sabbath observer to learn the lesson of the Sabbath. It takes effort and concentration to learn how to *call upon your own resources* and find your way back into the stream of life when you are drowning in loneliness.

There are other rules of the Sabbath that can serve as universal guidelines for dealing with loneliness. Work, for example, is not permitted on the Sabbath. Work is defined as the actual creation of something new—from striking a match to "create" a flame to writing a paragraph in creating a new idea. Intensive work on a term paper or a book or telephoning friends to make "dates," which can result in strain or effort and the frustration of disappointment—all of which would disturb the Sabbath rest—are not permitted. The theological undersprings of these practical consequences of observing the laws that govern the Sabbath are clearly described by I. Grunfeld in his book *The Sabbath*:

> All the week we have worked. All the week we have lived in the illusion that power in the world is in our hands. This has been the veil hiding from our eyes the truth that God is the source of all power.
>
> On Sabbath we have ceased from work. We have given up all *melakhah* [work] down to the last detail.

As a result, the veil has been lifted. Now we can glimpse in all its glory that truth which lies behind our purpose in the world.

This is the moment which must fill us with wonder and joy. It must awaken our hearts towards that spiritual contentment which is the secret of "Sabbath rest."

God is the source of power, but He wants us to share it with Him.

I suggest that these rules can serve as guidelines for the person who is mired in the depths of loneliness. You should not expect that exerting one supreme effort will pull you out of it. It is a slow, gradual process, step by step. Overexpectation can lead to the setback of frustration. Easy does it.

There is still another enlightening use of the concept of the Sabbath—the "Sabbath of History." Jewish theodicy affirms the belief in a Messiah. Evidence of his having come would be a radical change in the nature of man and society. It will be an era of peace and genuine fellowship. (The fact that this has not characterized the world in the last two thousand years is one of the reasons that Judaism does not believe that he has come, but is a matter for the future.) It is important to know that the more normative concept in Jewish lore is not the idea of the Messiah as a person, but as a period in history—the Messianic Era, or the Kingdom of God —at the end of time. It is often referred to as the "Sabbath of History." Its very name reveals its anticipated characteristics. Peace, fellowship, and contentment will derive from the fullest development of man's mind and the influence of his heart.

> The Kingdom of God, as pictured by the Jewish prophets . . . is an ideal society of nations on earth, living in accordance with the universal ethical rules of genuine justice, righteousness and peace.

The weekly Sabbath is often referred to as a foretaste of what that era will be like—not a period of undisturbed rest and unperturbed "peace of mind." Rather, it is a time that will challenge man to grow and reach his fullest potential; a time of intellectual stimulation and the regular practice of acts of kindness.

Again, such a teleological view of what can be, what we can bring about ultimately, has implications for what a person can do *now*, in preparation for that future and for what it means in his *today*. It has obvious implications for the power in a person who is lonely to pull himself out of it. The weekly Sabbath can be for a foretaste of what life can be again after one has found the way back.

5

A Journey of a Thousand Miles Begins with but a Single Step

The important thing is study, which leads to action.

— Talmud

Practice and theoretical study should be like blades of a pair of shears: neither blade is good for anything by itself, but they can cut by being in contact with each other.

— Arthur E. Morgan

. . . And now the single steps on the journey away from loneliness. However, first I remind the reader of the point I made at the end of chapter 2: *Ideas, properly understood, are actions—steps in shaping the mood of an individual*. The specific "exercises," habits, and disciplines to be detailed now should not take away from this truth. Clearly, just as one has to work at anything in life for it to succeed—from a business to a marriage to the writing of a book—a person has to work at conquering the depressing, life-consuming feeling of loneliness.

What can you do?

From the personal experiences of the authors themselves to the studies they describe, the literature on loneliness has a richness of insights and guidelines.

1. *Identify, recognize and face loneliness and its nuances for what they are*.

> It was helpful to me when William Saveller Jr. divided it into categories: Interpersonal—when you miss someone you love; Social—when you are excluded from a group; Cultural—when you feel cut off from a tradition and roots (the loneliness of immigrants and travelers); Cosmic—when you feel the universe is absurd; life is powerless; God is lost

(loneliness of the existentialist); and Psychological—when you feel absented from yourself and out of touch with your true nature (Terry Schwartz, *Bittersweet*).

People around you, relatives and friends, with the best of intentions may say to you: "Don't worry, it's not serious and you'll get over it soon." Do not pay heed to such unsophisticated advice. It *is* serious, and the first step in dealing with depression of loneliness is to recognize it for what it is: an illness of heart and mind which has to be treated.

2. *Don't get bogged down on little things. Remember the larger goal.*

He that lets
the small things of life bind him
leaves the great behind him.

3. *Maintain the confidence that you have the power to help yourself.*

The rabbis of the Midrash suggest that we view life —the world, as well as individual circumstances—as if everything is on a scale, with the two sides evenly balanced. What *you* do will tip the scale toward either achievement and success, on the one hand, or failure, on the other.

4. *Force yourself to do things.*

Seek the company of other people, even if you find it uncomfortable or awkward. Push yourself to renew experiences that gave you pleasure before the sadness set in: go to a concert, a ball game; play golf or tennis; read a book. Do not neglect physical exercise—the simplest home exercises, a regular morning walk.

5. *Take time for yourself alone.*

This is different from the depressing loneliness that, indeed, finds you alone so often. Consciously and deliberately set aside brief periods for reflection, thinking about yourself: "Why do I feel this way? How can I get out of it?" It is part of an effort we discussed in the chapter on the Sabbath that must be made to get in touch with yourself and draw on your inner resources.

6. *Don't make the mistake of thinking that the next person has it easier.*

A Jewish folk saying suggests that if you and all the people you know were to put your packs of trouble on a table and you were asked to pick the best of a bad lot, you would be happy to pick your own.

7. *Remember how much reality is determined by your own outlook on things.*

The rabbis of the Talmud put it this way: "Whoever sees things negatively is merely projecting his or her own feelings." As someone once put it, "I am old and have had many troubles, but a great many of them never happened."

The opposite is also true: a hopeful person creates openings to good experiences. Put your face in the contours of a smile—even if you have to force it—and it will induce a better feeling.

8. *Don't expect continuing uphill progress.*

One day you feel a little better. Don't be discouraged if, the next morning, it seems as hard as ever to get out of bed and start moving. The process is gradual—two steps forward and one backward, and then a few more, which lead to the light at the end of the tunnel.

9. *Don't look into the mirror too often, measuring your progress every minute.*

Getting better is a slow process, and all change and growth are gradual. I recall my own sense of feeling a little better from time to time, hoping, waiting expectantly. And then one day I realized how pleasant things were—all day. I had arrived, and a warm feeling of contentment enveloped me. I did not dwell on it, but accepted it gratefully and went ahead with the business of living.

10. *Above all, never use the excuse: "What I do doesn't make a difference."*

The worst thing—the greatest impediment—is the

attitude that you cannot help yourself. The opposite is true. No one experiencing loneliness will overcome it unless he or she plays a key role. All the assistances referred to earlier in this and other chapters are based on one premise: You have to be genuinely convinced that "I can do it!"

A new "ten commandements" for the lonely person? Not if you think that all of them are for you. Some may work for you; some may not. As you think about how you can be guided by them, other steps may suggest themselves to you as even more helpful. The key, again, is keeping at it.

A fundamental aspect of a productive, meaningful life is our relationship to others. It can only be achieved with a deeper understanding of the biblical verse "Love thy neighbor as thyself" (Leviticus 19:18). A commentary emphasizes the words *"as thyself."* Without proper self-respect, self-love, a mature relationship with yourself, you cannot develop respect, love, and a mature relationship with others.

One final emphasis: Remember that each person is a partner with God in making his or her life and the world an experience of love, purpose, and fulfillment. You have been given the freedom and power to *choose life*. Add years to your life by giving direction to your daily existence.

A hasidic story and a biblical verse tell it all:

A cynic wanted to "show up" a rabbi whose wisdom and piety were revered by his parishioners. One day, he confronted the rabbi in the presence of a number of his disciples:

"Rabbi," he said, "I have a bird in my hand behind my back. Demonstrate your wisdom, learned rabbi, tell us, is it dead or alive?"

His plan was that, if the rabbi said, "Dead," he would release the bird and let it fly away. If the rabbi said, "Alive," he would snuff out its life and present the rabbi with a dead bird.

With little hesitation, the rabbi looked at this challenger and said, "My son, the choice of life or death is in your hands."

I call heaven and earth as witnesses this day! Before you I have placed life and death, the blessing and the curse. You must choose life, so that you and your descendants will live." (Deuteronomy 30:19)

6

**Forethoughts . . . as Afterthoughts:
An Anthology on LONELINESS**

. . . . from notes gathered in preparing for this
book . . . and not quite fitting into the se-
quence of ideas which developed as the
volume took shape . . . . . .

. . . . Yet replete with insights and guidelines
for the lonely and not-so-lonely . . .

Pray that your loneliness may spur you into finding something to live for, great enough to die for.

Dag Hammerskjold

They are never alone that are accompanied with noble thoughts.

Sir Philip Sidney

When is man strong until he feels alone?

Robert Browning

I sat alone with my conscience
In a place where time had ceased.

Charles William Stubbs

Some night in his lifetime, everyone comes home to find a new guest there—disappointment . . . *If one is to come through difficult experiences unembittered, unspoiled, still a real person, one needs deep resources* . . . Not alone in such experiences as sorrow and failure does this need arise . . . Who does not need that? *But no one can get inner peace by pouncing on it*, by vigorously willing to have it . . . *Peace is an awareness of reserves from beyond ourselves*, so that our power is not so much in us as through us. [Emphasis added.]

Henry Emerson Fosdick

The gem cannot be polished without friction, nor man perfected without trials.

Confucius

Going up a mountain path one day, I met a mountaineer with an ax in his hand. I walked with him and asked him what he was going to cut. "I need a piece of timber to fix my wagon," he said. "I need *the toughest kind* of wood I can get. *That kind grows on top of the mountains where all the storms hit hardest.*

Archibald Rutledge

Difficulties are the things which show what men are.

Epictetus

"Are you not lonely?", asked a visitor of a lighthouse keeper on an isolated reef.

"Not since I saved my first man," came the swift answer.

Henry Emerson Fosdick

Our doubts are traitors,
And make us lose the good we oft might win
By fearing to attempt.

Shakespeare

Art thou in misery brother? Then I pray
Be comforted. Thy grief shall pass away.
Art thou elated? Ah, be not too gay;
Temper thy joy: this, too shall pass away.
Art thou in danger? Still let reason sway,
And cling to hope; this, too, shall pass away.
Tempted art thou? In all thine anguish lay
One truth to heart: this, too, shall pass away.

Paul Hamilton Hague

There is no grief which time does not soften.

Cicero

What time does, no wisdom can do.

Talmud

Life affords no higher pleasure than that of surmounting difficulties. . . . To strive with difficulties, and to conquer them, is the highest human felicity.

Samuel Johnson

Thou shalt forget thy misery, and remember it as waters that pass away.

Job 11:16

Come what may
Time and the hour runs through the darkest day.

Shakespeare

When you see that time resists (an idea) don't force it.
Midrash

Being alone, as such, is a markedly different experience from being lonely.
Clark E. Moustakas

Man is not alone.
Abraham Joshua Heschel

Solitude gives birth to the original in us, to beauty unfamiliar and perilous.
Thomas Mann

. . . Whereas the artist ultimately accepts his solitude, anxiety and mortality through his longings expressed in an external medium, the neurotic tries to overcome uncertainty and anxiety by perpetually manipulating himself in an effort to make his life perfect and predictable—which is an unfinishable, crippling enterprise.
Michael Vincent Miller

Solitude is a return to one's own self when the world has grown cold and meaningless, when life has become filled with people and too much of a response to others. *Solitude is as much an intrinsic desire in man as [is] his gregariousness.* [Emphasis added.]
Clark E. Moustakas

Silence is not nothingness or the absence of sound. It is a prime condition for human serenity and the natural environment of contemplation. A life without regular periods of silence is a life without essential nourishment for both the spirit and the functioning intelligence.

Norman Cousins

. . . That's one of the troubles with the world today . . . Everybody thinks that something should be done right away. And that's not true. Maybe we could do with a lot of non-doing. Maybe the thing to do now is nothing. But, you know, the journalists and the people who, they say, control public opinion are always calling upon something to be done. I wish we could call a moratorium upon actions for the next ten years; then we might be saved.

Mark Van Doren

It is not enough for me to be able to say, "I am." I want to know who I am . . . what is the meaning of my being. My quest is not for theoretical knowledge about myself . . . but deserves and evokes an eternal Amen.

Meditation - High Holiday
Service of Reform Synagogues

In a century in which so many of the mentors of the public mind—from the psychiatrists to the ad-men—speak to us in terms of "what we owe ourselves," may there not indeed have been a slackening of devotion compared with those days, not so distant, when *what man owes to God and his neighbor was a common theme of human discourse*. [Emphasis added.]

Adlai E. Stevenson

The longest journey
Is the journey inward
Of him who has chosen his destiny,
Who has started the quest
For the source of his being.

Dag Hammerskjold

A man lives by believing in something, not by debating and arguing about many things.

Thomas Carlyle

There is a realm of time where the goal is not to have but to be, not to own but to give, not to control but to share, not to subdue but to be in accord. Life goes wrong when the control of space, the acquisition of things of space becomes our sole concern . . . *Inner liberty depends upon being exempt from domination of things*. [Emphasis added.]

Abraham Joshua Heschel

I believe in the sun even when it is not shining.
I believe in love even when not feeling it.
I believe in God even when He is silent.

> Inscription in a Cologne celler
> where Jews hid.

Real beauty is a ray which emanates from the holy of
holies of the spirit and illuminates the body, as life
comes from the depth of earth and gives color and
scent to a flower.

> Kahlil Gibran

Work is the other component, not work as a compul-
sive activity in order to escape aloneness . . . but
work as creative in which man becomes one with nature in the act of creation.

> Eric Fromm

It is the greatest of failures to do nothing because you
can only do a little. Do what you can.

> Sidney Smith

Rabbi Isaac said:
If a man says to you, I have toiled and I have not found
  —do not believe him.
I have not toiled and I have found
  —do not believe him.

I have toiled and I have found
  —believe him.

Talmud

Naught is given 'neath the sun,
Naught is had that is not won.

Swedish Hymn

No man lives by denying life.

Andre Malraux

All beginnings are difficult.

Midrash

Withdraw unto yourself and look, and if you do not find
yourself beautiful as yet, do as the creator of a statue
that is to be made beautiful: he cuts away here; he
smooths there . . . until he has shown a beautiful face
upon the statue.

Plotinus

The great virtue of man lies in his ability to correct his
mistakes and continally to make a new man of himself.

Wang Yang-ming

Don't be disgusted, don't give up, don't be impatient
. . . but after a fall, return again.

Marcus Aurelius

The worst of particularities is to withdraw yourself, the worst ignorance is not to act.

Charles Pegy

Man is summoned to God to be a conqueror. And Judaism approves of a man's quest for the stars.

Joseph B. Soloveitchik

For those who will fight bravely and not yield, there is a triumphant victory over all the dark things in life.

James Allen

Man can be as big as he wants. No problem of human destiny is beyond human beings.

John F. Kennedy

We are potentially all things; our personality is what we are able to realize of the infinite wealth which our divine human nature contains hidden in its depths.

W. R. Inge

Courage and perseverence have a magical talisman, before which difficulties disappear and obstacles vanish into air.

John Quincy Adams

Not everything that is faced can be changed; but nothing can be changed until it is faced.

James Baldwin

To regret one's own experiences is to arrest one's development.

Oscar Wilde

It is ignorance of one's own errors that makes one ready to see errors of others.

Solomon Schechter

There is resiliency in the soul of man and he may be down to bleed a while and return refreshed.

Heywood Campbell Brown

Arise then, freeman, stand forth in thy world. It is God's world. It is also thine.

Josiah Royce

A preacher driving along the road sees one of his parishioners clearing up a poor stony field.

"That's a fine job you and the Lord have done cleaning up that rocky field."

The man looked up, saying, "Thank you, Parson. I wish you could have seen it when the Lord had it all to Himself."

Adlai E. Stevenson

Perhaps the most valuable result of all education is the ability to make yourself do the thing you have to do, where it ought to be done, *whether you like it nor not.* [Emphasis added.]

Thomas H. Huxley

It is a time for education in the obvious rather than investigation of the obscure.

Oliver Wendell Holmes

. . . No one has yet suggested opening a "spare parts" department for worn-out or defective human emotions. *The repair of a "broken" heart from the loss of a loved one may present far more of a therapeutic challenge than the technical skills needed for a heart transplant operation.*

James J. Lynch

Most folks are about as happy as they make their minds to be.

Abraham Lincoln

To me, there is in happiness an element of forgetfulness. You lose yourself in something outside yourself when you are happy, just as when you are desperately miserable you are intensely conscious of yourself, [you] are a solid lump of ego weighing a ton.

J. B. Priestly

If I were a godfather wishing a gift on a child, it would be that he should always be more interested in people than himself. That is a *real* gift.

Sir Compton Mackenzie

First become a blessing to yourself so that you may be a blessing to others.

Samson Raphael Hirsch

Worrying has been defined as the act of borrowing trouble from the future for present-day consumption; and courage has been defined as the act of borrowing hope from the future for present day consumption.

Max Artzt

Let us be of good cheer, remembering that the misfortune hardest to bear are those which never happen.

James Russell Lowell

Nothing is as good as it seems beforehand.

George Eliot

When trouble comes, our self-consciousness is heightened and our vision is apt to become warped. *Troubles are like infants—they grow by nursing.* We think that we are alone, are called upon to suffer, to bear disappointment or the death of a loved one, and that evil has befallen us alone. Maturity leads us to maintain an emotional balance with the realization that others are suffering too, and that some are in a far worse plight. There is an oriental proverb worth recalling when we feel overcome with self-pity and consumed with resentment: *"I was without shoes and I murmured, 'till I met a man without feet."* [Emphasis added.]

Saul Teplitz

Man should never attempt to bear more than one kind of trouble at a time. Some people bear all the troubles they have had, all they have not and all they expect to have—all at once.

Edward Everett Hale

Nothing in life is to be feared. It is only to be understood.

Marie Curie

The paradoxical situation with most people is that they are half asleep when awake and half awake when asleep.

Erich Fromm

The day will happen whether or not you get up.

John Ciardi

God that gives the wound may give the remedy. This is one day but tomorrow is another.

Miguel de Cervantes

God prepares the cure before the illness.

Talmud

Everyone must have two pockets so that he can reach into the one or the other, according to his needs. In his right pocket are to be the words, "For my sake was the world created" and in his left, "I am dust and ashes."

Hasidic

Nothing can bring you peace but yourself.

Ralph Waldo Emerson

I know of no more encouraging fact than the unquestionable ability of man to elevate his life by conscious endeavor.

Henry David Thoreau

Unfortunately, in seeking liberty many try to throw off the "yoke" of a spiritually guided life. . . . so "freedom" is sought to "do as we please."

The Rebbe of Lubavitch

That we have the possibility of seeing with our eyes is no power in us; but is in our power that we make a good or bad use of our eyes.

Pelagius

Your life is what your thoughts make it.

Marcus Aurelius

A little knowledge that *acts* is worth infinitely more than much knowledge that is idle.

Kahlil Gibran

They can because they think they can.

Virgil

Be willing to have it so. Acceptance of what happened is the first step to overcoming the consequences of any misfortune.

William James

By accepting reality—taking things as they are and not as I want them to be—by doing all this, rare knowledge has come to me, and are powers as well.

A patient's letter to C. J. Jung

Despair is the conclusion of fools.

Benjamin Disraeli

A person entirely without shortcomings and frailties would hardly be lovable. Only a person with some shortcomings has understanding for the shortcomings of others. And only when there is this understanding is there charity and leniency and warmth between men.

Hans Margolis

. . . the goal of human effort is to be able . . . to follow what the heart desires without transgressing what is right.

Walter Lippmann

If a man will begin with certitudes, he shall end in doubt, but if he will be content to begin with doubt, he shall end in certitude.

Francis Bacon

Life is not like physical things. Life itself keeps life going. If you use a car a lot, the car wears out and your legs get weak, but if you walk a lot, your legs get strong. The non-living wears itself out by work, but the living builds itself up. That's one of the great differences between life and non-life.

Albert Szent-Gyorgi

We would be better to think of joy and intense aliveness instead of happiness.

Erich Fromm

Contentment comes not in anything weighed, measured or counted, but only in things hidden from the eye.

Talmud

Feeling and thoughts are our own, while possessions are alien and often treacherous to the self. *To be is more essential than to have. Though we deal with things, we live with deeds.*

Abraham Joshua Heschel

People who want by the yard and try by the inch should be kicked by the foot.

W. William Wurtz

He who sings frightens away his ills.

Miguel de Cervantes

God dislikes melancholy and depressed spirits. Joy is the cure of illness caused by melancholy.

Hasidic

Sound sleep by night, sturdy and ease
Together mix'd, sweet recreation
And innocent, which most does please . . .
With Meditation

Alexander Pope

Something attempted, something done
Has earned a night's repose.

Henry Wadsworth Longfellow

Without fullness of experience, length of days is nothing. *Where fullness of life has been achieved, shortness of day is nothing.* . . . This experience of fulfillment through wholeness is the answer to the brevity of man's days.

Lewis Mumford

Men are born to succeed, not to fail.

Henry David Thoreau

That day which you fear as being the end of all things is the birthday of eternity.

Seneca

Life is a voyage that is homeward bound.

Herman Melville

God does not die when we cease to believe in a personal deity, but we die on the day when our lives cease to be illuminated by steady radiance, renewed daily, of a wonder, the source of which is beyond all reason.

Dag Hammerskjold

Dear God, give us the strength to accept with serenity the things that cannot be changed. Give us the courage to change what can and should be changed. And give us the wisdom to distinguish one from the other.

Thomas C. Hart

I am quite ready to acknowledge . . . that I ought to be grieved at death, if I were not persuaded that I am going to other gods who are wise and good (of this I am certain as I can be of any such matters), and to men departed who are better than those whom I leave behind. And therefore, I do not grieve as I might have done, *for I have good hope that there is yet something remaining for the dead*. [Emphasis added.]

Socrates

Seeing the world as we do, a lonely, insecure, transitory place, we look within it for places of security and evidences of permanence and these we find . . . in the abstract, in compassion, and in the concrete in human relationships of love and deep acceptance. We know that death is always near, and that each man goes his separate way to death. But we find in this knowledge not only separateness but also union of the generations. Death is the place, the experience that brings together generations that have gone before and that will come.

Jacob Neusner

May the blessing of light be on you, light without and light within.

May the blessed sunlight shine upon you and warm your heart till it glows like a great peat fire, so that the stranger may come and warm himself at it, and also a friend.

And may the light shine out of the eyes of you, like a candle set in the windows of a house, bidding the wanderer to come out of the storm.

And may the blessing of the rain be on you—soft, sweet rain. May it fall upon your spirit so that all the little flowers may spring up, and shower their sweetness on the air.

And may the blessings of the great rains be on you, may they beat upon your spirit and wash it fair and clean, and leave there many a shining pool where the blue of heaven shines, and sometimes a star.

And may the blessing of the earth be on you—great round earth. May you ever have a kindly greeting for them that pass as you're going along the roads. May the earth be soft under you when you rest out upon it, tired at the end of a day and may it rest easy over you where, at last, you be out under it.

May it rest so lightly over you that your soul may be off from under it quickly, and up and off and on its way to God.

And now may the Lord bless you and bless you fully.

Old Irish Blessing

We thank You . . . for Your miracles which are daily with us, for Your continual wonders.

Daily Prayer Book